# MONEY MANAGEMENT CARIBBEAN STYLE

## BY

## NIGEL ST. HILL

## Life and Money Management Coach

Published by Nigel St. Hill
www.moneyandabundance.com

ISBN: 978-1522774754

# ACKNOWLEDGMENTS

I wish to express gratitude to Vernon Williams who was instrumental in having me pursue studies in Credit Management.

I am deeply thankful to my sister, Myrna who has been a tower of strength and support over the years... to my brothers, Cedric, Clinton, Colin, Carlton and to my daughters, Gail and Nicole for their encouragement.

I extend my gratitude to Jennifer Cruickshank and Jennifer St. Hill for their review and helpful feedback in the preparation of this book and my dear friend and supporter Ina Pickering.

I am thankful to all of my students, teachers and clients who have contributed to my personal growth and understanding.

Finally, I would like to express my love and gratitude to my mother, Elita and father, Deighton.

# MOVING FROM TRANSACTION TO TRANSFORMATION

## Contents

*"Until one is committed there is hesitancy, the chance to draw back, always ineffectiveness, concerning all acts of initiative (and creation).*

*There is one elementary truth, the ignorance of which kills countless ideas and splendid plans: that the moment one definitely commits oneself then providence moves too. All sorts of things occur to help one that would never otherwise have occurred.*

*A whole stream of events issues from the decision, and meetings and material assistance which no person could have dreamed would have come his/her way.*

*Whatever you can do or dream you can begin it.*

*Boldness has genius, power and magic in it.*

*Begin it now."*

GOETHE

# COMMITMENT TO
# CONTINUOUS IMPROVEMENT

*Throughout the duration of this programme:*

*I am committed to change.*

*I am committed to letting go of all that no longer serves my highest good.*

*I am committed to changing the old tapes in my mind.*

*I am committed to walking into a new reality.*

*Signed.........................................*

*Date........................................*

# Introduction

## Life Changes

Today, being aware of the ongoing changes in every aspect of our lives has become an important task for our survival and our continued well-being. We see companies and organizations collapse because they have not been able to change their ways of thinking and behaving. Individuals experience frustration when time is not spent anticipating changes and responding to the need for change.

We have seen more changes in the last decade than in the previous one hundred years. It is this rapid change that heightens our anxieties.

Change is infinite and we must always expect fluctuations when dealing with what we own. We must also expect changes in our loved ones, jobs and positions in life. We evolve from child to parent, dependent to independent and sometimes back to dependent. It therefore would be in our best interest to flow with these moves and re-arrangements in life. This will require a paradigm shift.

# The Paradigm Shift

A paradigm, in a general sense, is the way we see the world – not in terms of our visual sight, but in terms of perceiving, understanding and interpreting.

If we want to make relatively minor changes in our lives, we can, perhaps, appropriately focus on our attitudes and behaviors. But, if we want to make significant change, we need to work on our basic paradigms.

There is always another way of looking at any situation or challenge that is presented to us. What you see is what you get.

www.moneyandabundance.com

# Paradigms:

A simple way to look at paradigms is to see them as maps. Each of us has many, many maps in our head which can be divided into two main categories. Maps of the way things are, and maps of the way things should be. We interpret everything we experience through these mental maps.

We seldom question their accuracy; we're usually unaware that we have them. We simply assume that the way we see things is the way they really are or the way they should be.

Our attitudes and behaviors grow out of these assumptions. People all over the world seem to believe that other people see life the same way they do, or at least, they should. To try to change our attitudes and behaviors does very little good in the long run, if we fail to examine the basic paradigms from which those attitudes and behaviors flow. The more aware we are of our basic paradigms, maps or assumptions, and the extent to which we have been influenced by our experiences, the more we can take responsibility for those paradigms, examine them, listen to others and be open to their perceptions, thereby getting a larger picture and a far more objective view.

# How to Change Your Money Paradigm

As a child growing up I was bombarded with all types of messages about money, or more correctly the negative aspects of money. So often I heard, "Money is the root of all evil." "You can't change human nature." "Save for a rainy day." "The rich get richer and the poor get poorer." I am quite sure that you are saying yes to most of these phrases.

When I realized the impact that this programming had on my life, I started to pay closer attention to what I was thinking and feeling about this very emotive subject called money.

How often have you heard the saying, "a coin has two sides?" Similarly, the subject of money has two sides: (1) plenty of money which carries the feeling of freedom and ease that plenty of money can provide: and (2) lack of money, the feeling of fear and disappointment that the thought of lack of money induces.

When you are able to consciously make the correlation between the thoughts that you have been thinking about money, the way you feel when you think those thoughts and the money that flows into your experience, you can make the necessary changes to improve your financial situation.

So often we assume that when we say "I want more money," that we are speaking positively about money. But when you are speaking about money and have a feeling of fear or discomfort as you speak, you are not speaking about "plenty money," you are speaking about the "absence of money." And the difference is very important, because the first statement (as shown in 1 above) brings money and the second keeps it away.

It's of value for you to become aware of how you are really thinking and more important, feeling about money. If you are thinking or saying things like:

"Oh, that is a very beautiful bed - but I can't afford it," you are not allowing in the abundance that you desire. The feeling of disappointment that is present as you acknowledge that you cannot afford it is your indicator that your thought is pointed more toward the lack of what you desire than toward the desire itself.

To effect the positive change as it relates to your relationship with money, you must be prepared to be transformed into a new person. This change will be reflected in your thinking and your actions, and will ultimately lead to a change in your results.

To change your outer world, you must change your inner world. It is imperative that you believe that you have the capacity to make the necessary changes to your financial future. And I know you can.

## So, Here Are 3 Steps To Get You Started:

Acknowledge what others around you may be saying about money matters. You then make the following statement, "I understand that the people around me hold different views about money, spending, saving, giving money, receiving money, and it is not necessary for me to understand their opinions or perspectives."

Develop some positive statements, for example, "financial abundance comes to me easily and effortlessly and I accept it now." "I love the idea that more money gives me more choices. I will buy that car and I will live in a new neighborhood." "I am increasingly magnetized to money, prosperity and abundance." Repeat these statements often so that they become second nature.

Develop a positive expectation attitude as you look towards the future as shown in the example below.

"I understand that money will not necessarily appear instantly in my life with the changing of my thinking, but I do expect to see a steady improvement as a result of my conscious effort to think better feeling thoughts. I am certain about that."

So begin today by first becoming aware of what you are thinking and saying negatively and change that to something more positive that will bring the desired results.

# WEEK 1

# What Is Your Current Financial Picture?

**The First Step Is To Know Where You Are Now In Relationship To Money.**

| Strategy |
| --- |

## Get Clear about Income, Expenses, and True Needs

In this strategy we are going to get practical since you must become very clear about where you are right now in relation to your income, expenses and true needs.

# Step 1: Get An Overview Of Your Financial Picture.

Develop a realistic monthly plan that addresses important needs and wants.

Keep a list of unmet wants and needs that can be addressed in the future.

Check to see where you might be feeling a sense of deprivation, the roots of which may go back to early family history.

Low self-esteem and having been emotionally and physically abandoned as a child are patterns that may cause impulsive spending, which ultimately sabotages financial well-being. How many times do you go out and buy something when you feel depressed, angry, or emotionally empty?

The monthly plan should include amounts set aside for future periodic expenses, like new tires for the car or vacations, to prevent these expenses from ending up on a credit card.

# Step 2: Keep Track Daily Of What Is Spent. Record Keeping Helps On Many Levels.

First, tracking expenses allows us to feel more in control of our money, rather than the other way around.

Second, jotting down expenses helps keep us more conscious about spending. Being conscious helps you to express the intention to have more money.

Third, having a realistic plan usually makes us feel less anxious. Feeling more relaxed creates a flow of creativity and optimism.

With increased clarity about spending patterns and motivating feelings, each month's expenses become easier to plan. Realistic decisions can be made about letting go of expenses that drain money without giving value in return.

## Where Are You Spending And Getting In Money?

If you have multiple streams of income, look at which are making money and which are not generating money. Put your focus on what is working and let go of those that are not.

www.moneyandabundance.com

Look at what other opportunities are available and possible.

- Where are you leaking money?
- How much money is required to move the business forward?
- How much money do you need per month?
- What else do you have to do to bring in more money?
- How much do you want to make per hour?
- How many clients do you want to see per week?
- How is your business model structured?

# Prepare a Twelve Month Financial Projection

## What Is Your Vision For The Future?

You need to look at money without fear and coming from a point of love and gratitude.

- How would life be different if I got comfortable with money? Be specific with what is holding you back.
- How much money do you want to make?
- How many clients do you need to get to generate that amount of money?
- Does the business model support that?
- Look at your lifestyle and make a list adding the dollar amounts to them.
- Why do you want to make that amount of money?

In answering these questions and reviewing your responses, you have just created a realistic picture for your financial journey. I now encourage you to move towards the doors of abundance and prosperity, and let go the paths of scarcity and lack.

www.moneyandabundance.com

# WEEK 2

## Recognizing Poverty Consciousness

Have you ever wondered why there is so much poverty in a world overflowing with wealth? Have you noticed how many individuals have difficulty manifesting abundance?

Poverty is the opposite of abundance. Therefore, a discussion of poverty may help us understand how we can manifest abundance.

One of the reasons poverty is so widespread is that poverty consciousness exists in the world. People see poverty on television and in the movies, in magazines as well as in neighborhoods. If the pictures and stories are graphic enough, we believe them, discuss them, and think about them. These images are implanted in our conscious minds and then transferred deep into our subconscious minds.

In addition, newspapers, magazines, and other media daily report these conditions as reality. The media's justification for continuing to focus on negative reports rests on the premise that this is real, so we must continue to see it and dwell on it.

If we see poverty, we believe it to be real. If we believe it to be real, our thoughts, feelings, words and actions continue to create it. As we continue to create more apparent poverty in the world, many people begin to fear that perhaps it will touch their own lives. Fear brings more poverty into reality. Therefore we talk about it more... It is a vicious cycle that is self-perpetuating.

Choosing between poverty and abundance is a good way to start breaking this cycle. Remember that to choose one means that you must let the other one go. Monitor your thoughts and beliefs, and then decide just how willing you are to let the negative ones go.

## Steps To Break The Cycle:

## Your beliefs about money determine how you attract it, spend it, and relate to it.

## <u>Uncovering Your Core Beliefs</u>

1. When you were growing up what did you learn about money?
2. Who taught you that life is supposed to be a certain way?
3. What do you believe about yourself?
4. What do you think you deserve?
5. Look at a current situation in your life involving money and ask, "What beliefs would someone have had to create this situation?" Make a list of several possibilities. When you have discovered the right one you will know by how you feel inside.
6. Write below a new belief about money that you would like to have.
7. Do you believe it is possible to make money doing what you love?
8. Or do you believe that making money requires hard work and struggle?

If there is something you want and you do not yet have it, you may have a belief that is keeping you from having it. Within every belief you are living out there is the seed of opposite belief that you have not yet manifested. Within the belief that you don't deserve money lies its opposite – the belief that you **DO** deserve money. As you take your attention away from the negative belief and begin activating the positive one, you change what you experience.

**Finally, here are samples of new belief statements that you could begin to use:**

1. I believe in my unlimited prosperity.
2. I choose beliefs that bring me aliveness and growth.
3. My beliefs create good things for me.
4. I deserve abundance.

**JUST PUT THEM INTO PRACTICE.** Add your own to the above list.

**Note: It often helps to write your new belief statement on a sheet of paper and put it where you will see it frequently, e.g. wallet or purse.**

# WEEK 3

## Understanding Resistance

We humans have the power of spontaneous action, doing old things in new ways, changing and restructuring our lives and our behavior. Yet an innate resistance limits this possibility; this resistance is based upon our most fundamental physical and psychological structures, connected to the larger universe and to the ways we learn and adapt to our environment when young.

Resistance is nothing more than precepts in one's mind that oppose change. Courage, on the other hand, is a quality within one's mind that encourages the individual to face opposition or advancement without fear. By choosing courage over fear you will move in the direction that you want.

Dropping the resistance creates a new kind of openness that enables you to attract a new reality into your life.

You are like a river. You go through life taking the path of least resistance. We all do – all human beings and all of nature. You may try to change the direction of your own financial flow. And you may succeed for a time. But eventually you will find that you return to your original behavior and attitudes. This is because the law of nature dictates that you take the path of least resistance.

The good news is that you can change your fundamental underlying structures. Just like engineers can change the path of a river by changing the structure of the terrain so that the river flows where they want it to go, you can change the very basic structure of your financial blueprint so that you can create the life that you want. Furthermore, once a new basic structure of allowing abundance is in place, the path of least resistance cannot lead anywhere except in the direction you really want to go.

It is only by becoming aware of the resistance that the necessary changes can be made. As you begin to feel freer regarding the expenditure of money, doors will open, people will come to assist you, refreshing and productive ideas will occur to you, and circumstances and events will unfold.

Here is how to identify resistance:

1. Start by acknowledging that there is resistance.
2. Be there when it happens, when the resistance arises.
3. Observe how your mind creates it, how it labels the situation, yourself or others.
4. Look at the thought process involved.
5. Feel the energy of the emotion.
6. By being fully present, the unconscious resistance is made conscious.
7. Now you are presented with a choice; you can continue to resist or you can relax and allow in the natural flow of abundance.

**Here is an example from my own experience in September 2010.**

On September 9th 2010, I attended the Quarterly Social of The Barbados Coalition of Service Industries held at the 3 Ws Oval.

I won a prize of dinner for two at one of the leading south coast hotels here in Barbados. Needless to say, this prize was a saving, since I didn't have to pay for a birthday celebration.

We have a tendency only to look for the winning of the lottery as an indication of our abundance. However, there are several ways of allowing the universe to give you what you want. Be open to them.

## How to Change Resistance to Abundance

Take an honest look at the way you were raised.

What were the main beliefs about money that were instilled in you from early childhood?

- What examples did your parents set in the home through their actions? What emotions were most prevalent?
- How did you feel as a child in your home environment?
- Can you detect any harmful beliefs that were embedded within you?

To what extent have you completely liberated any damaging beliefs that were instilled in you? Without judging yourself, just notice how fully independent you are of the way you were raised.

## Have You Been Able To Free Yourself From Your Childhood Blueprint?

For the time being, stop trying to "do" anything to money and instead turn your attention inward. As you focus on your awareness, see if you can choose to perceive money as a symbol of generosity and freedom rather than scarcity and contraction. Be willing to see money in a new light. Starting right now, declare for yourself that, regardless of your current financial state, money is a source of freedom and generosity in your life.

www.moneyandabundance.com

As you do this, it will become clear what your money blocks are. You'll see the subconscious holding patterns coming to the surface that have likely kept you locked in your current financial state year after year.

## What Obstacles Do You See?

**Is one of them fear?**

**Do you still have the belief that you're not good enough to have more money?**

**Can you cut through the momentum of fear, negative beliefs, harmful emotions or addictions?**

**Can you settle into a quiet acceptance of money in your life as it currently stands? Let the resistance to the presence of money in your life completely fade away.**

As you do this, now go deep into your imagination. Imagine the money is a symbol of freedom. Imagine everyone you know having more than enough money and feeling completely liberated by its presence in their lives. Imagine that money fulfils the needs and dreams of countless people on this planet. Your basic needs are met and you can meet the needs of countless other people.

One of the main ways that poverty consciousness shows up in our lives is in the statement, **"I can't afford it."**

Instead of saying **"I can't afford it,"** use the following statement. **"I am choosing to use my resources in other ways, right now."**

Make wise conscious choices when making purchases, not out of fear, which cuts off the flow.

**Now commit to this newfound understanding of the purpose that money has in your life at all times.**

www.moneyandabundance.com

# WEEK 4

## Releasing - How to Let Go Of Your Old Beliefs about Money

Releasing is simply saying, preferably out loud, a statement of acceptance that a particular belief or judgment is no longer true to you. I say "no longer", because the statement is tied to a negative belief you have had that is causing you problems. It is a powerful verbal method to free your mind from the negative influences that seem to bombard both from without and within.

The technique works as though you are holding your belief tightly in your hand, then you put your arm out and let it go! It's rather like dropping it through a trap door. The use of a statement of belief, or affirmation is an attempt to implant that belief in your mind.

You may have to say it in different ways, since the inner self may have the idea implanted in different ways.

You have a belief based on a perception and you make a judgment that becomes part of your inner mindset.

The releasing strategy is a tool you can use to lift out and let go of blocks and limits in your mind. You might say Releasing is a lever to lift off the weights that are dragging you down, or holding you back, in any area of life.

We busily judge events, situations, and people as either good or bad, and immediately put them accordingly into our subconscious data banks. The negative beliefs seldom end up helping us, and often hurt us as we project them out into our current and future relationships and actions.

You must let go of whatever perception or inner belief is causing the problem.

Your negative beliefs and fears about yourself can come up and ruin your life at any time if they're allowed to get rooted in your inner mind. Since we are not taught as children to release, or to let go of unhelpful beliefs, we generally have to want to transform our life into something else to want to have a better life.

Take a moment and look at your childhood messages. How did your parents spend money? Did they buy things for themselves? Did they enjoy their money, or did they struggle to have enough? Did they talk freely with you about how much they earned, or was money a forbidden topic? How did they spend on you? Did you feel that your wishes counted? Can you see a connection between the way you relate to money now and the relationship your parents had to money? Did your parents allow themselves to spend and earn money in ways that brought them aliveness, happiness, well-being, and self-love?

To release the past, look at the stories you have been telling yourself and others about your childhood and money. Do you tell people that you had abundance or scarcity? Perhaps you tell about the times when there wasn't enough food. Or perhaps you tell tales about how parents spent money, but didn't buy things for you. Start by looking at the aspects of your personal history you emphasize with others. For every experience you had, you also had an experience that was nearly its opposite. There were times you had wonderful meals and times you got things you really wanted that had value to you.

What financial history would you like to have? Begin to make a new history for yourself. Reconstruct your childhood with memories of prosperity and getting what you wanted. What would you like to tell people your childhood was like? For instance, you might want to tell people, "My parents spent money very wisely. Money was not an issue in our family, we always had enough." As you say this you will probably remember times when money really wasn't an issue and you really did have enough.

Here now are two examples which I invite you to use as you begin your practice of releasing and letting go.

**Here now are two examples which I invite you to use as you begin your practice of releasing and letting go.**

**Examples of releasing statements:**

1. I release my belief, perception and judgment that I am not in control of my life if I don't have more money.
2. I release my belief, perception and judgment that I have no power if I don't have as much money as someone else has.

Just remember to practice, practice and practice again until you form the new habits that you want to see in your life.

---

# WEEK 5

## Rhythm - Letting Money Flow

As you gain a better understanding of creating abundance, you will recognize that money flows in and out, like the ocean waves. You will experience times when the tide is in and times when the tide is out. Some months you will receive more money than usual, and some months you will have more bills than normal. Some weeks your business may be booming, and other weeks you may have very few customers.

There is a natural rhythm to money, just as there is a natural cycle to everything in life. Every business has an ebb and flow. Every person has cycles in life, times when money is coming in more than it is going out and times when it is going out more than it is coming in. Your challenge is not to go up and down emotionally with the natural ebb and flow of money in your life; use these natural cycles in a way that further builds prosperity.

There are four basic states of flow you might experience; calm, when money is coming in and going out in equal amounts; flow, when much more money is coming in than going out; ebb, when much more money is going out than coming in; and flat, when no money is flowing in or out. Money represents an exchange of energy between you and the outside world. It represents the energy going out from you and the energy coming back to you.

Everyone looks forward to the flow, when more money is coming in than going out. You experience this many times during the month. When you receive your paycheck or any sum of money before you spend it, you have created a flow. Start by acknowledging that you already have a flow in your life, and that what you want is even more days when more money is coming in than going out. If you acknowledged yourself every time you had even one day of more money coming in than going out, you will find the flow increasing in your life. If you have reached a level where you consistently have an excess of money coming in, congratulate yourself. Take a moment to appreciate and acknowledge your accomplishment.

There are some challenges at this level. One of the challenges when more money is coming in than going out is to keep your expenses far enough below your increased wealth that when the natural ebb comes you will still be able to pay your bills. It is easy at any level of wealth to spend more than you have and keep yourself broke. Some people don't experience abundance because they spend all the money they make or more, or increase their monthly expenses so much when their income goes up that they don't have enough money to meet their bills when the tide goes out. Those who feel wealthy are usually spending less than they make.

When more money is coming in than going out, when you are getting more business or money than expected, it is a challenge to continue to ask for more. If you say, "This is too much; if it continues I won't be able to handle all the business, responsibility, or work," you may put the brakes on more tightly than you expect and you might find the money or business less than you want. When you feel that you are inundated by business, work, opportunities, or money, don't put on the brakes. Challenge yourself to ask for more. Indulge in unlimited thinking and expand your imagination about what is possible for you to have.

When you are in an upward cycle, keep opening to even more. Realize that as more comes in you will develop new processes, forms, and structures in your life and business to handle it. You may end up hiring help, changing what you do, and being able to reach more people. As you become more abundant, one of your challenges will be to handle all the choices, opportunities, and abundance that come to you. You will be challenged to grow, reach more people, get your work out in a larger way, and accept more responsibility, power and abundance.

## Here Is an Example of Telling "My New Story" About Money

It is fun to imagine a lot of money flowing to me. I can see how my feeling about money affects the money that comes to me. I am happy to understand that with practice I can control my attitude about money, or about anything for that matter. I notice that the more I tell my story of abundance, the better I feel.

I like knowing that I am the creator of my reality and that the money that flows to me is directly related to my thoughts. I like knowing that I can adjust the amount of money that I receive by adjusting my thoughts.

Now that I understand the formula for creating, now that I understand that I do get the essence of what I think about, and, most important, now that I understand that I can tell by the way I am feeling whether I am focused upon money or lack of money, I feel confident that in time, I will align my thoughts with abundance and money will flow powerfully into my experience.

## Exercise

One day during the course of the week, place $50.00 in your pocket, wallet or purse and mentally purchase as many items as you want. Just the simple act of noticing how many things you could purchase in this one day with the $50.00 you are carrying with you would dramatically alter your financial point of attraction. That one simple process is enough to show you actual tangible results in your attraction of money. Mentally spend your money and imagine an improved lifestyle, deliberately conjure a feeling of freedom by imagining what it would feel like to have a large amount of money at your disposal.

## Exercise

Having thoroughly read through the above material, write your new story.

# WEEK 6

## Receiving – Completing the Money Cycle

To create many flows of money in your life, learn to give and receive freely. You want to receive as well as give. Many of us love to give to others, yet it is harder to allow ourselves to receive from them. You empower others by letting them give to you, for they then have the opportunity to demonstrate their abundance. People feel good about themselves when they give you something that you can use and appreciate. If no one could receive, no one would be able to give, which will block the flow of energy necessary to create abundance.

Do not see it as selfish for you to receive; see it as the completion of the circle of energy. The more you are open to receive, the more you can give. Receive money from people, and do so with warmth and graciousness. Imagine ten times the amount of money someone gives you coming back to them every time you receive money. As you envision success for other people, you increase your own magnetism to prosperity.

Be open to receiving with gratitude and grace. If you receive a check for fifty dollars, thank the creator for it, rather than saying, "this is not enough." So many people receive money and say, "I don't know how I'm going to make it last; I wish I had received more." They take the amount and make it less, and less will come next time.

If you receive money with an image of more coming, with a feeling of joy and thanks, you create more ways for the creator to give you prosperity.

Be open to receiving from any source that honors your integrity and be willing to get what you ask for. Sometimes people look for hidden strings or for the flaws in what they are receiving.

Imagine that you are looking for a used fridge. You decide that you want this fridge at a very affordable price, a fridge that is in excellent condition. You have a clear idea in your mind what you want. Then one day you find a fridge that meets all your conditions; and cost even less than you imagined. Rather than being pleased because it seems so perfect, you wonder if something is wrong!

You need to trust your ability to create something ideal; affirm your power to create what you want. As you master the process of manifesting, you will often receive things that seem too good to be true, so enjoy what you create.

Think of all the sources from which you allow money to come to you (e.g. your job, income from investments, family and friends to name a few). What other ways might you receive income? Include ways that seem improbable, such as anonymous cheques, notification from the bank that you have more than you thought in your account, or an unexpected refund. Be as outrageous and imaginative as you can. Then ask yourself, "Am I willing to receive from new sources?" If you are, and I am sure that you are, ask the universe to send you money through a new channel in the next several weeks. Be willing to acknowledge it when it comes, and congratulate yourself for creating new ways to receive abundance.

# Exercise Receiving

1. Make a list of as many things as you can think of that you would like to receive.

2. Go over each item. Ask yourself if you are truly willing to receive it? Are there differences in your answers for different items?

3. Take something you feel most open to receive. Observe what the feeling "open to receive" is like. Does it have a feeling in your body, in your emotions or thoughts?

4. Take something you don't feel as open to receive from your list above. Remembering how it felt to be open to receive, play with your thoughts, feelings, and physical sensations until you feel more open to receive your object.

# About the Author

Nigel St. Hill is the founder of http://www.moneyandabundance.com and author of the book Money Management Caribbean Style and several eBooks including 12 Secrets to Creating Money and Abundance Caribbean Style, 8 Money Management Secrets for Caribbean Women, Creative But Practical Ways to Save money, 8 Simple Ways to Live a Healthy Abundant Lifestyle and 7 Steps To Becoming An Empowered Single Woman.

He is a certified Life and Money Management Coach helping people who are ready to uncover their path to Love, Happiness and Abundance by providing them with empowering informational products and life and money management coaching.

He worked with Cable & Wireless (now LIME) as their Credit Manager and had the honour of becoming the first person in the Caribbean to be qualified in Credit Management. Nigel conducted extensive training programs for employees of Cable & Wireless in Barbados, Grenada, St.Lucia and St.Vincent. He also wrote the first Standard Credit Management Procedure for Cable & Wireless Barbados.
In addition to Credit Management, he worked for a number of years in the hospitality industry as a night auditor and was Credit Administrator for the Harris Group of Companies.

Always one for sharing his knowledge and experiences with the world, he has written numerous articles in the local newspapers and magazines on Change Management, Money Management and Credit Management. He also wrote articles for In the Zone Magazine and Caribbean Success University. He currently writes a monthly article for Bajandiaspora, a USA based online magazine. Many readers have also benefited from his writings through Ezinearticles, Selfgrowth.com, Pinterest, Tumblr and LinkedIn.

With a thirst for continued learning, in 2011 he completed the Adult and Continuing Education and Teaching Certificate (TVET) Train- the-Trainer Course and in 2015, Nigel received the Small Business Association award for the most outstanding performance in the Maximizing Social Media for Small Business Entrepreneurship Training Series.

A solution oriented individual with many talents and gifts, his desire is to share the knowledge, experiences and insights that he has gained as a result of his own transformation.

He currently facilitates the "Unlock Your Future Program" for fourth and fifth formers in three of Barbados' Secondary Schools. This program is geared to prepare students for both life and the world of work.

Contact Nigel St. Hill – Life and Money Management Coach

email:nigel@moneyandabundance.com

Tel: (1 246) 228-1155
Cell: (1 246) 244-4784

Like us on Facebook:
www.facebook.com/MoneyandAbundance

Free tips on:
http://www.moneyandabundance.com

http://www.twitter.com/nigelsthill

Skype: nigeldst.hill

---

Well, congratulations!

I certainly hope that I was able to provide you with the tools and techniques that will move your personal life and business forward.

I thank you for the opportunity to be of service to you and wish you continued success.

Nigel St. Hill – Life and Money Management Coach

---